Date: 6/29/18

BR 534 BOO
Boothroyd, Jennifer,
Vibrations make sound /

Vibrations Make Sound

by Jennifer Boothroyd

first step nonfiction

Lerner Publications · Minneapolis

LERNER

SOURCE

Expand learning beyond the printed book. Download free, complementary educational resources for this book from our website, www.lerneresource.com.

The images in this book are used with the permission of: © Stockbyte/Thinkstock, p. 4, 10, 21; © Sombat Muycheen/Shutterstock.com, p. 5; © iStock/Thinkstock, p. 6, 7, 8, 14, 15, 17; © Wavebreak Media/Thinkstock, p. 9, 13; © Ratchapol Yindeesuk/Shutterstock.com, p. 11; © Digital Vision/Thinkstock, p. 12, 18; © Pavel L. Photo and Video/Shutterstock.com, p. 16; © Tyler Olsen/Shutterstock.com, p. 19; © iStockphoto.com/smartview27, p. 20; © F1online/Thinkstock, p. 22.

Front Cover: © mfron/istock/Thinkstock

Main body text set in ITC Avant Garde Gothic Std Medium 21/25.
Typeface provided by Adobe Systems.

Lerner Publications Company
A division of Lerner Publishing Group, Inc.
241 First Avenue North
Minneapolis, MN 55401 USA

For reading levels and more information, look up this title at www.lernerbooks.com.

The Cataloging-in-Publication Data for *Vibrations Make Sound* is on file at the Library of Congress.

ISBN: 978–1–4677–3910–8 (LB)
ISBN: 978–1–4677–4689–2 (EB)

LC record available at https://lccn.loc.gov/2013044229

Manufactured in the United States of America
5-45447-16073-3/2/2018

Table of Contents

Sound is everywhere.

Sound is what we **hear**.

You can't see sound.

Sound moves through the air.

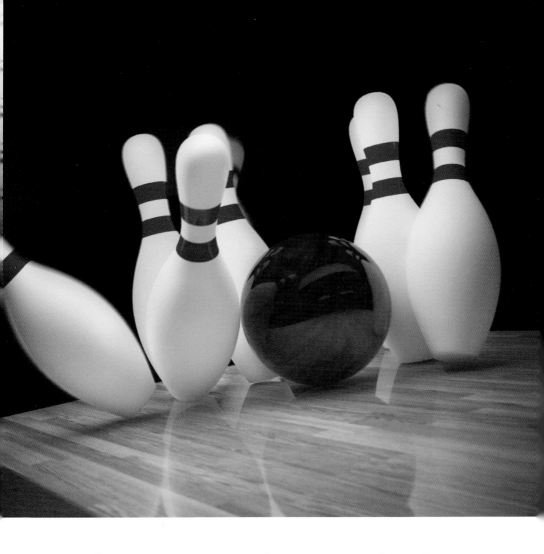

Some sounds are short.

Some sounds last longer.

Sounds can be quiet.

Sounds can be loud.

Sound is made when something **vibrates**.

Rubbing things together makes vibrations.

Vibrations are types of movement.

Different vibrations make
different sounds.

A hit makes vibrations.

You can hear a bat hitting a ball.

Air makes vibrations.

You can hear air blowing through a whistle.

Can You Make Sound?

Clap your hands.

Hands can vibrate against each other.

Clap your hands harder to make a louder sound.

Your throat vibrates when you speak.

Say a few words.

You can make quiet sounds.

Rub your shoes on the floor.

Knock on a door.

Tap your pencil on your desk.

What other sounds can you make?

Glossary

hear – to catch sound with your ears

sound – vibrations that move through the air

vibrates – moves quickly back and forth

vibrations - small, fast movements back and forth

Index